MIDDLE EAST LEADERS™

AYATOLLAH KHOMEINI

Edward Willett

rosen
central™

The Rosen Publishing Group, Inc.,
New York

Published in 2004 by The Rosen Publishing Group, Inc.
29 East 21st Street, New York, NY 10010

First Edition

Library of Congress Cataloging-in-Publication Data

Willett, Edward, 1959–
Ayatollah Khomeini / by Edward Willett.— 1st ed.
    p. cm. — (Middle East Leaders)
Summary: Examines the life and leadership skills of Ayatollah
Khomeini, who established the "ideal Islamic state" in Iran
and encouraged Muslims worldwide to demonstrate against
non-Islamic nations.
Includes bibliographical references and index.
ISBN 0-8239-4465-4
1. Khomeini, Ruhollah—Juvenile literature. 2. Heads of state—
Iran—Biography—Juvenile literature. [1. Khomeini, Ruhollah.
2. Islam—Biography. 3. Iran—History—1979–]
I. Title. II. Series.
DS318.84.K48W55 2003
955.05'42'092—dc21

2003009897

Manufactured in the United States of America

CONTENTS

HERO OR TYRANT?

■ Ayatollah Khomeini is shown here praying among other Islamic faithful. Khomeini had spent most of his adult life studying the Koran and teaching. Only in his sixties did he become politically outspoken.

Ayatollah Ruhollah Musavi Khomeini died in 1989 at the age of eighty-six. His Islamic revolutionary leadership, however, still casts a long shadow across world affairs. For many people in Iran and other

Muslim countries, he is a hero. He was the man who brought down a corrupt monarchy. He drove out "the Great Satan" (America). He also placed the religion of Islam at its rightful place at the center of both political and everyday life in Iran.

In the West, he is remembered as a fanatical dictator. He turned Iran from an island of stability in the Middle East to a supporter of terror and an exporter of revolution.

But before the 1979 revolution in Iran and especially before the taking of hostages by students who stormed the U.S. Embassy in Tehran, most Americans had probably never heard of Khomeini. The man with the loosely wound black turban, white beard, and fierce, piercing gaze seemed to have come out of nowhere.

He didn't, of course. Every Iranian knew who he was before the revolution. He had been the spiritual leader of the opposition to the reign of the shah (king) for almost twenty years. He spent fifteen years in exile in Turkey, Iraq, and France, but his speeches and writings were constantly circulated.

Khomeini was seventy-six years old when he was made leader of the new Islamic Republic of Iran. The last ten years of his life made him world famous, but the more than seven decades he lived before that shaped him into the political and religious force he became.

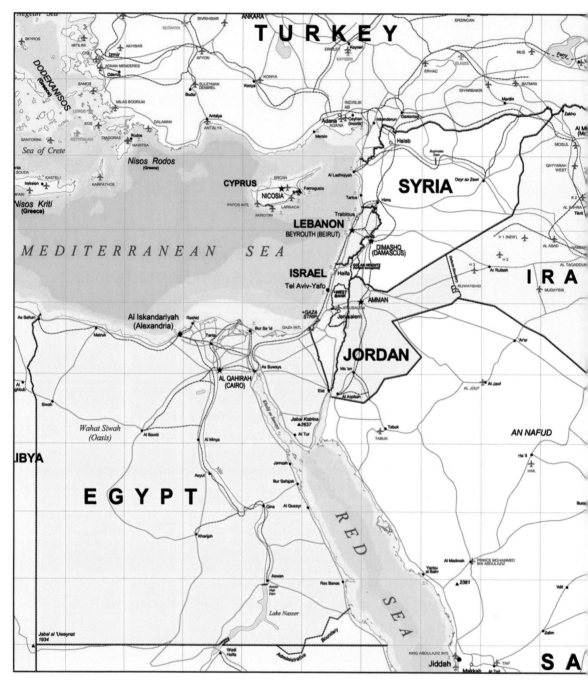

Iran is one of the largest countries of the Islamic Middle East. Many Westerners see Middle Eastern people as Arabs. This is not true. Iran has a majority of Persians, with the next largest ethnic group being Azeri. Arabs make up less than 5 percent (2002 figures) of Iran's population.

CHAPTER ONE
KHOMEINI'S CHILDHOOD

■ This photo shows the birthplace of Ayatollah Khomeini, in the city of Khomein, Iran. Visitors from Tehran often drive the three and a half hours (200 miles [322 kilometers]) to visit the mud and brick home of Iran's Islamic revolutionary leader.

Ruhollah Musavi Khomeini was born on September 24, 1902, in the town of Khomein in central Persia, as Iran was called until 1935. Khomein was a town of about 2,000 in that year. The town was not poor, despite its small size. It lay on one of the main trade routes between the ports on the Persian Gulf to the south and Iran's capital city, Tehran, to the north. The winter snows of the nearby Zagros Mountains watered the surrounding farmland every spring.

Ruhollah (the name means "inspired by God") was born in a two-story house on the village's eastern edge. Like most of the homes, it was made of mud bricks plastered over with a mixture of clay and straw. The house was built around three courtyards and had two watchtowers.

Its size was a testament to the respect given to Ruhollah's family within the town. The family originally lived in Neishabur in northeastern Iran and migrated in the late 1700s to northern India to give religious instruction and guidance to the large Shiite population living there.

Sometime in the mid-nineteenth century, Ruhollah's grandfather, Seyyed Ahmad Musavi Hindi, left India. He went to Najaf, Iraq, the site of a Shiite shrine. ("Hindi," a nickname relating to Ahmad's time in India, was passed down to his descendants; even Ruhollah used it on occasion.) In Najaf, Ahmad accepted an invitation to move to Khomein and became the town's religious teacher.

Ahmad was well off. In 1839, he bought the 43,000-square-foot (3,995 square meters) property where Ruhollah would be born sixty-three years later. Over the next few years, he bought more property in other villages in the district. He also bought an orchard and caravansary (an inn for passing caravans) in Khomein.

Ahmad's third wife, Sakinah, had three girls and a boy. The boy, Mostafa, was only thirteen when Ahmad died. Following the family tradition, he, too, studied religion. Mostafa eventually traveled to Najaf himself. There,

Ayatollah Khomeini

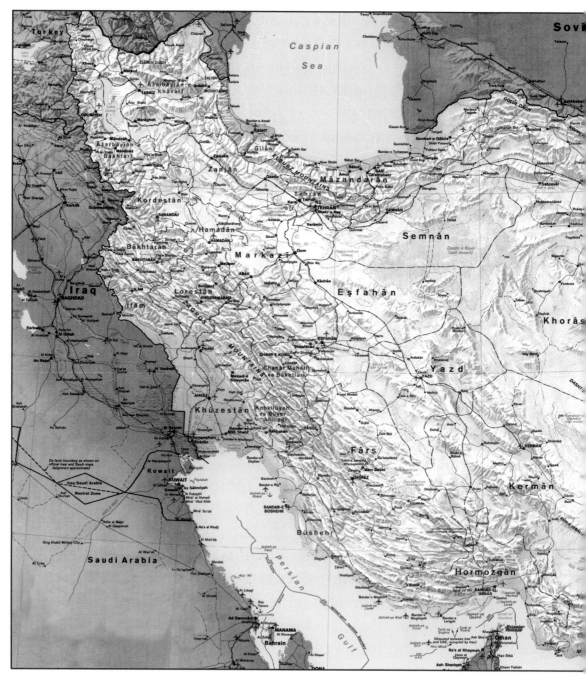

■ This map of Iran shows a mountainous country well positioned near water sources used for natural resources and commerce. Iran's most valuable natural resource is its oil reserves. Today, it is one of the leading producers of oil in the region.

10

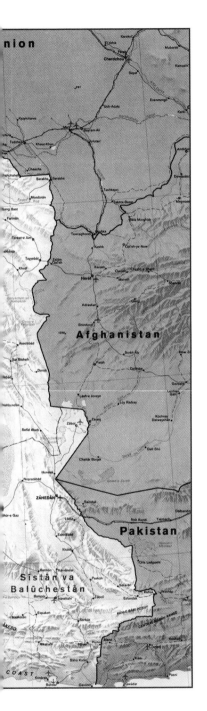

he and his wife, Hajieh Agha Khanum, had their first daughter. In 1894, Mostafa was given permission to issue his own interpretations of religious law, and he returned to Khomein. There he had two more daughters (names unknown) and three sons, Morteza, Nurredim, and Ruhollah.

In March 1903, less than six months after Ruhollah's birth, Mostafa was shot and killed while traveling from Khomein to Arak. Ruhollah's brother Morteza, eight years old at the time, wrote in a memoir published in the magazine *Pasdar-e Islam* in 1988 that Mostafa was killed by two local khans (chieftains) because he was on his way to Arak to ask the provincial governor to stop the khans from oppressing the people. His killers were eventually caught; one died in prison, and the other was beheaded after most of the Khomeini family traveled to Tehran to press for justice (leaving Ruhollah, still a toddler, and his sisters behind in the care of servants). The family returned to Khomein in May 1905.

Life and Early Education in Khomein

Ruhollah, his mother, and many other family members and servants all lived in the Khomeini home. The provincial governor's deputy also had his offices on the first floor of an old part of the building. On the second floor stood his guards' living quarters. Ruhollah didn't mind the crowded home; he often spent all day in the streets. Just as often he came home wearing torn, dirty clothes, his body covered in an assortment of cuts and bruises. Strong and athletic, he was a local champion at leapfrogging, wrestling, and other sports.

One of Ruhollah's favorite games was *dozd-o-vazir* ("the thief and the vizier"). This was a make-believe game in which a thief is captured by guards and taken to the king. The king then orders his vizier to have him punished. "Even as a youngster, my father always wanted to be the Shah," Khomeini's son, Ahmad, said in a 1982 interview with Dr. Hamid Algar, now a professor at the University of California, Berkeley.

There was plenty of excitement without make-believe. The Lurs, the local tribesmen, often raided Khomein. In his memoir, Morteza recalled rushing home from a New Year's Day (March 21 in Iran) visit with friends to find police shooting at mounted tribesmen from the family watchtowers. Another time,

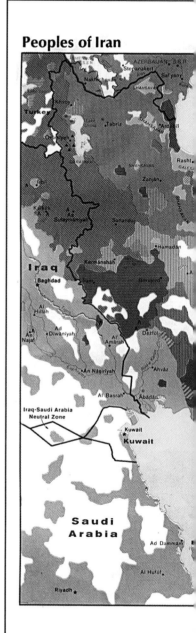

Peoples of Iran

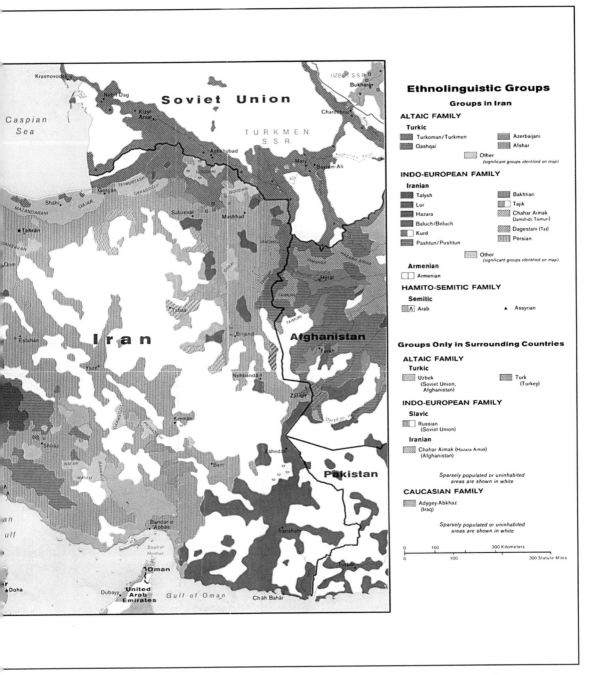

Ethnolinguistic Groups

Groups in Iran

ALTAIC FAMILY

Turkic

- Turkoman/Turkmen
- Qashqai
- Azerbaijani
- Afshar
- Other *(significant groups identified on map)*

INDO-EUROPEAN FAMILY

Iranian

- Talysh
- Lur
- Hazara
- Baluch/Beluch
- Kurd
- Pashtun/Pushtun
- Bakhtiari
- Tajik
- Chahar Aimak (Jamshidi, Taimuni)
- Dagestani (Tat)
- Persian
- Other *(significant groups identified on map)*

Armenian

- Armenian

HAMITO-SEMITIC FAMILY

Semitic

- Λ Arab
- ▲ Assyrian

Groups Only in Surrounding Countries

ALTAIC FAMILY

Turkic

- Uzbek (Soviet Union, Afghanistan)
- Turk (Turkey)

INDO-EUROPEAN FAMILY

Slavic

- Russian (Soviet Union)

Iranian

- Chahar Aimak (Hazara Aimak) (Afghanistan)

Sparsely populated or uninhabited areas are shown in white

CAUCASIAN FAMILY

- Adygey-Abkhaz (Iraq)

Sparsely populated or uninhabited areas are shown in white

| 0 | | 100 | | 300 Kilometers |
| 0 | | 100 | | 300 Statute Miles |

Many different ethnicities comprise Iran's population. The ethnic majority is Persian, but dozens of other groups live in small and large pockets throughout the country.

The Constitutional Revolution

Beginning in the mid-1890s, common people, merchants, and clergy began objecting to the Iranian government's actions. In December 1905, a major demonstration took place in Tehran after the prime minister punished some merchants for raising the price of sugar. Then, in the summer of 1906, the shah's guards fired into a crowd of demonstrators and killed a seminary student. Shortly after, 14,000 people, mostly clergymen, sat in protest within the British Embassy's grounds. (Britain and Russia wielded major influence over Iran at the time.) The demonstrators stayed there for a month. They demanded that Iran write a new constitution and create a representative assembly.

In October 1906, the first National Consultative Assembly (Majles-e Showra-ye Melli in Persian, or Majles for short) convened. In December, the shah signed the Constitutional Law. This was the first Iranian law set by the civil government rather than by clerics, who set religious laws. The shah died shortly thereafter. But in 1907, the new shah, Mohammad Ali Shah, abolished the Majles and arrested the leaders of the constitutional movement. That led to riots. In 1909, Mohammad Ali Shah was overthrown and replaced by his eleven-year-old son, Sultan Ahmad.

Among Mohammad Ali Shah's supporters was the powerful clergyman Sheikh Fazlollah Nuri, who opposed giving the Majles the power to make laws because he believed only God had that right. The government's only purpose, in his view, was to enforce *shari'a*, Islamic religious law. After Mohammad Ali Shah was deposed, Sheikh Fazlollah was tried, condemned, and executed. A new Majles convened. Iran appeared poised to become a democratic state modeled on those of western Europe, while the clergy had lost much of its authority.

Such was the political environment in which Ruhollah Khomeini began his education. Ruhollah Khomeini later claimed Sheik Fazlollah as one of his heroes.

Ruhollah and his brothers picked up rifles to defend the family home.

When he was seven, Ruhollah started attending the local school, or *maktab*. There, boys memorized the alphabet, the Koran (the Islamic holy book), and religious stories while sitting on rugs on the floor. Mispronouncing a word was grounds for a beating.

Ruhollah began to learn the history of the Shiite faith. The Shiites see themselves as historically oppressed. They believe it is the duty of those wronged to take revenge. Ruhollah also read or heard many of the great works of Persian literature. He loved poetry and memorized hundreds of different verses. He continued to write poetry off and on throughout his life.

From the maktab, Ruhollah moved on to a new secular school recently opened by the constitutional government. There, he studied arithmetic, geography, history, and science. Private tutors continued his Islamic studies.

In 1918, when Ruhollah was sixteen, his mother and aunt (who had helped to raise him) died in a cholera epidemic. The following year, Ruhollah entered the *madraseh*—the seminary.

CHAPTER TWO
KHOMEINI THE STUDENT

A group of nomads travel along a dirt road near Sultanabad-Arak. The young Khomeini would have also used a horse to travel this rural road during his years as a student in the madraseh.

Khomeini first studied religion in Isfahan, a town near Khomein. After a few months, though, he moved to Sultanabad-Arak. This was home to one of the principal scholars of the time, Sheikh Abdolkarim Haeri.

Most clergy competed for influence within the seminary. Therefore, they made sure that their followers accompanied them wherever they went. But even though 300 students regularly attended his talks, Haeri often walked about unaccompanied. This simple style seems to have rubbed off on Khomeini, who practiced it later in life.

Khomeini took his studies very seriously. Once Khomeini even scolded Haeri for disturbing his concentration by talking too loudly while teaching in the courtyard.

When a student in the madraseh commits himself to studying religion, he undergoes a ceremony. His skullcap and short jacket are exchanged for the turban, long coat, and floor-length cloak worn by members of the clergy. He is then known as a *talebah*, or "seeker." Khomeini received his turban in 1922. Shortly after, he moved to Qom, 90 miles (145 kilometers) south of Tehran. He did so to follow Haeri, who had himself moved there in 1921.

The clerical community in Qom had invited Haeri in the hopes that his presence would help Qom regain its former importance as a center of learning. They hoped to make Qom an alternative to Najaf, from which the Shiite leaders had been expelled recently by the British authorities.

Sure enough, clergy from Sultanabad-Arak and many other cities soon joined Haeri in Qom. The city eventually became the spiritual capital of Iran—and Khomeini's true home. As he told a group of visitors from Qom in Tehran in 1980, "Wherever I may be, I am a citizen of Qom, and take pride in the fact. My heart is always with Qom and its people." Khomeini began studying at a madraseh called Dar al-Shafa, or "hospital," because it had been used as one for many years.

A Day at the Madraseh

A Muslim clerical student studies the Koran.

In Islam, the *madraseh* (place of religious learning) is considered as important as the mosque, the place of worship. What is taught in the madrasehs hasn't changed much since they were first established in the eleventh century: Islamic law (*shari'a*), Arabic grammar and rhetoric, theology, jurisprudence, and logic. Students begin by memorizing important texts; later they are encouraged to seek the meaning of the texts and discuss the various interpretations of them.

On a typical day, students rise before dawn. After ritual washing and the morning prayer, they head to the first lecture. This might last for an hour or two. Afterward comes breakfast, then more lectures. In the afternoon, students are paired off to discuss any questions they might have.

Lecturers sit on the floor or on a low stool. The students sit cross-legged on the floor. Students choose how many lectures to attend; some hire outside tutors as well. Many students spend much of their time reading poetry, history, or philosophy or memorizing the Koran.

Traditionally, Shiite religious studies are divided into three levels. The first level takes about four years. Afterward, a student can become a *mas'aleh-gu*, or "explainer of problems." This is the lowest rank of the religious hierarchy. A few of these move a step further up in the hierarchy to become a *va'ez*, or preacher. Those few students who move on to the second level of learning begin to teach first-level students. While teaching, they continue to focus their own studies on Islamic law, linguistics, and logic.

Those who finish the second stage can leave the madraseh and become mullahs in charge of local mosques. Khomeini reached this point in the mid-1920s. However, he continued on to the third level, similar to graduate work in a U.S. university. At this level, there are no set texts; instead, students study legal issues that concern them and develop their own opinions and ideas.

A handful of third-level students become so knowledgeable in a particular area of the law that they are given the right to issue their own interpretations on that topic. Fewer still know enough about all of Islamic law that they are given permission to issue their own interpretations on any topic. At that point, the student has become a full-fledged *mojtahed*, or jurist; he may also be called *hojjat al-Islam*, which means "proof of Islam."

Two Branches of Islam

Islam is divided into two main branches: Sunnism and Shiism. The story of how the branches formed comes from the origins of the religion itself. Islam was founded by the prophet Muhammad. When he died in 632, his family believed that his cousin and son-in-law, Ali (the Prophet's

Ayatollah Khomeini

■ This illustration depicts the prophet Muhammad (c. 570–632) reciting the Koran to onlookers. At the age of forty, and for the next twenty years, Muhammad brought his message of Allah to the people. He practiced the way of life that he was preaching to others to live.

first convert), should become the next *imam*, or leader of the faithful. Other followers, however, said the Prophet had left no instructions. Therefore, they reasoned, the imam should be chosen from the wider community of believers. They took the leadership, forming the Umayyad dynasty.

In defiance, the Prophet's grandson, Hussein, and a band of fewer than a hundred followers, including women and children, decided to fight for justice. Hussein and his band were wiped out in a battle in Karbala (today, part of southern Iraq) in 680.

The majority of today's 1 billion or so Muslims are Sunni Muslims, whose ancestors accepted the Umayyad dynasty. Those who believe that Ali should have been named leader became Shiite Muslims ("Shiite" comes from the Arabic *shiat Ali*, meaning "the party of Ali").

The majority of Shiites are called Twelvers, because they recognize twelve imams, beginning with Ali. The twelfth, called the Hidden Imam, disappeared in 873 but will return as the Mahdi (Messiah). Each imam, Shiites believe, was infallible, could foresee future events, and could intercede between people and God.

Ayatollah Khomeini

■ Ruhollah Khomeini is shown here at the age of twenty-five, before being elevated to Ayatollah ("sign of God"). Khomeini enjoyed his studies and, when he began to teach, quickly found a following of students.

Worldwide, only about 15 percent of Muslims are Shiite, so in most Muslim countries they are in the minority. In Iran, however, where Twelver Shiism became the state religion in the sixteenth century, they are the majority.

Khomeini the Teacher

By the time he was twenty-seven years old, Khomeini had developed his own circle of students. He had also developed his own style of teaching. Normally, lectures were conducted as a kind of argument between teacher and students. Ayatollah Ja'far Sobhani, one of Khomeini's students, is quoted in Hamid Ruhani-Ziyarati's 1981 book, *Barrasi va tahlil az Nahzat-e Emam Khomeini* (A Study and Analysis of Imam Khomeini's Movement), as saying Khomeini "put forward a topic in a decisive manner, first explaining other opinions and then his own before looking for arguments. He never introduced issues that were unclear in his own mind, preferring to do his homework, and reflect upon topics before discussing them."

Regarded as "learned, intelligent, chaste and pious," and a handsome bachelor to boot, Khomeini caught the attention of the wealthy Ayatollah Mirza Mohammad Saqafi in Tehran. Khomeini's friend Lavasani knew Saqafi. He suggested to Khomeini that he should be thinking about getting married—and pointed out that Saqafi had two eligible daughters.

Khomeini requested the hand of Saqafi's fifteen-year-old daughter, Qodse Iran (known to her family as Qodsi), in 1929. She refused him, but then, as she explained in a 1994 interview that appeared in the

Ayatollah and Marja' Taqlid

A *marja'* studies a text in a library.

In Shiism, very learned mojtaheds may eventually be seen as *marja' taqlid* (*marja'* for short), which means "source of emulation." A marja's authority is accepted by both ordinary people and lesser clergymen.

Each believer is expected to choose whom he or she will recognize as a marja'; he should be the most learned mojtahed of his time and of impeccable moral character. Most people rely on the advice of their local mullahs. They in turn rely on others who are higher up in the religious hierarchy. The ideal is a single marja', recognized by all believers, but that has been rare over the years.

In 1906, the clerical leaders who signed the new Iranian constitution were honored with the name *ayatollah*, which means "sign of God." At first, only marja's were referred to as ayatollah. By the 1920s, however, the term had begun to be used for any great religious leader, and a new term, *ayatollah al-ozma*, or "grand ayatollah," was coined for all marja's.

newspaper *Resalat*, she had a dream in which the prophet Muhammad's daughter, Fatimah, told her to marry him. The next day, she told her parents she had changed her mind.

Many Iranian men took more than one wife, but not Khomeini. His marriage to Qodsi was to last sixty years.

CHAPTER THREE

FROM MYSTIC TO POLITICIAN

■ When Reza Khan rose to become the new shah of Iran in 1926, his celebrations exceeded what had been seen in Iran for decades. Shown here is the Persian infantry on parade during the new shah's review of the military.

F or the next several years, Khomeini lived quietly, teaching classes and continuing his own studies. Among the subjects he chose were the rather unusual studies of philosophy and mysticism.

Mysticism is the belief that direct knowledge of God can be attained through individual insight or inspiration. Mainstream Shiite thought holds that the only path to God is through total obedience and devotion. Therefore, mystics have always been subject to suspicion.

Khomeini's most influential teacher in the field of mysticism was Mirza Muhammad Ali Shahabadi. Shahabadi taught Khomeini mysticism for seven years. He was also one of the few clergymen who actively opposed the policies of Reza Shah. Reza Shah ruled Iran as shah (king) from 1925 to 1941.

Reza Shah's attempts to modernize Iran during the late 1920s and 1930s had turned many members of the clergy against him. His new criminal and commercial codes were based on those of the French, not on Islamic beliefs. All of the training the clergy had had, he said, no longer qualified them to practice law. Instead, a new law school and examination system were set up. New secular (nonreligious) schools drew students from the religious schools. This further undercut the clergy's influence and income.

In the 1930s, following the conduct of Mustafa Kemal in neighboring Turkey, Reza Shah's policies became even more upsetting. He ordered men to wear European hats and forced women to discard the traditional Islamic head covering. But since opponents to his policies could expect to be imprisoned or even executed, the clergy, though outraged, for the most part did nothing. Traditionally, Shiite clergymen separate themselves from political decisions. Also, a tradition called *taqiyya*, or "dissimulation," allows Shiites to even deny their faith, if that's the only way they can continue to practice it.

The Ascent of Reza Shah

Reza Khan Mir Panj was a commander of the 8,000-man Cossack Brigade that carried out British orders in Persia. In February 1921, Reza Khan and the Cossack Brigade helped Seyyed Zia Tabataba'i overthrow the government of Premier Sepahdar Rashti. Ahmad Shah appointed Tabataba'i prime minister and Reza Khan commander of the Cossack Brigade.

Reza Khan Pahlavi sits on the Persian throne during the ceremony to appoint him shah on December 16, 1925.

The new government arrested opposition politicians and journalists. It also began to try to modernize the country through land reform, the building of modern schools, and financial reorganization. Reza Khan claimed his sole role was to keep law and order; he said he didn't have any political ambitions. Nonetheless, he became prime minister in 1923 when Ahmad Shah offered the post to him. Ahmad Shah then left for Europe and never returned to Iran.

Reza Khan convinced the clergy he would protect their honor and promote Shiism. With its support, that of the army, and that of the British, he convinced the Majles to dissolve the former Qajar dynasty. He convinced them to also make him leader of a provisional government until a new "elective" constituent assembly could decide the future government of Iran.

The elections to create that assembly were probably rigged; in any event, of 260 deputies, 257 voted to create a new Pahlavi dynasty. In 1925, Reza Khan became Reza Shah.

One of Khomeini's students, Mohammad Sadeqi Tehrani, told the magazine *Yad* in a 1986 interview that Khomeini explicitly referred to taqiyya when asked by a senior ayatollah why he hadn't tried to stop the partial demolition of a mosque to make way for a road. Khomeini also knew he hadn't yet advanced far enough in the religious hierarchy to challenge the shah. Still engrossed in his religious studies, he might not even have considered such a thing.

He was now studying the work of Mullah Sadra. Sadra's book, *Four Journeys*, Khomeini later said, helped him understand the mystical path a man had to walk if he were to become a "Perfect Man." This Perfect Man would be one who could guide society toward perfection through the establishment of the right policies and a government of absolute justice.

Khomeini himself wrote many books on the mystical understanding he gained. However, because many Shiite clergymen considered such thinking heretical, he was very careful about exactly how he said things. Some of his books were not published until after the 1979 revolution.

Did Khomeini eventually see himself as having become the Perfect Man? One former student, Ayatollah Haeri, now a leading Iranian scholar of Western and Islamic philosophy, thinks so. If so, it might have contributed to the enormous self-confidence with which Khomeini pursued his aims in later life. Through the 1930s, 1940s, and 1950s, Khomeini was mostly content to concentrate on his teaching. However, he was certainly both aware of, and interested in, political events.

Changes Come to Iran

Though widely seen as a dictator, Reza Shah wasn't removed by a popular uprising. Instead, he was forced out in the autumn of 1941 by an invasion of his country. This was at the height of World War II (1939–1945). The Allies (Britain, France, the United States, and others) were concerned about his pro-German leanings. They wanted to open a new route to Russia. The Allies swept through Iran, took power away from Reza Shah, and sent him into exile in Egypt, where he later died. They handed the crown to Reza Shah's twenty-one-year-old son, Muhammad Reza.

Several years of freedom followed for the Iranian people. This was partly because Muhammad Reza's personality was quite different from his father's. He was not a brutal dictator. He wanted to help modernize his country. Allied soldiers in the country also helped the Iranian people. The democratic ideals of the Constitutional Revolution were revived. Many new newspapers appeared. Political prisoners were released. A new Communist political movement, the Tudeh Party, was formed. It became popular among university students. To discourage its growth, religious activity was encouraged. Traditional dress was no longer banned.

The Clergy Turn Political

Conservative clergymen began to hope that some of Reza Shah's early secular changes could be reversed under his son, Muhammad Reza. Secular influences, however, continued to erode religious power. Many women didn't want to go back to wearing a veil. Newspapers, art,

Iranian citizens hold a newspaper denouncing the influences of Russia over the Iranian government. Muhammad Reza wanted to modernize the country after his father was deposed. His close ties to outside governments brought about corruption and foreign encroachment into Iranian political affairs.

music, and films displayed alternative ways of thinking. A growing minority saw religion as an ancient superstition from which they had been freed.

In 1946, Ayatollah Borujerdi emerged as the sole marja' taqlid of the Shia. Under his leadership, the clergy generally had a friendly relationship with the state. Khomeini, a firm believer in religious authority and clerical unity, supported Borujerdi. Khomeini also sympathized with a radical fundamentalist group, the Feda'iyan-e Islam ("fighters for Islam"). This group wanted to establish an Islamic state. It felt justified in using violence, especially assassination, to attain that goal. Navvab Safavi, founder of the Feda'iyan-e Islam, regularly visited Khomeini's home.

In 1942, Khomeini made an important political statement. He did so anonymously, in a short book called *Kashf al-Asrar* (The Discovery of Secrets). In it, he attacked secularism and the legacy of Reza Shah, whom he called "that illiterate soldier."

Most interesting, he set down his first thoughts about what an ideal Islamic state would be like. He said that it didn't matter whether the country was a monarchy or a republic, as long

■ Muhammad Reza Shah Pahlavi (shown here at his wedding in 1951) was willing to work with Western powers following World War II. As his rule of the Iranian people became harsh, members of the clergy became increasingly critical of his rule.

as all laws contrary to shari'a were abolished and people who spoke out against shari'a were harshly punished.

In 1949, Dr. Mohammad Mosaddeq founded the National Front. Its primary goal was the nationalization of the oil industry, then owned by the British. It also wanted to reduce the powers of the shah. In 1951, Mosaddeq became Iran's prime minister.

Khomeini's friend Kashani supported Mosaddeq for a time. However, Mosaddeq would not support the Feda'iyan's demand to apply shari'a law. Kashani withdrew his support and went on to help General Fazlollah Zahedi—with the help of the United States Central Intelligence Agency (CIA) and the British—overthrow Mossadeq in August 1953.

Through all this upheaval, the orthodox clergy, led by Borujerdi, remained quiet. Though Khomeini favored the Feda'iyan, he always stopped short of criticizing Borujerdi's position in public.

His continuing political silence meant Khomeini was seen as a great teacher rather than a political figure in the early 1950s. A religious historian, Mohammad Sharif Razi, writing

■ Khomeini's sympathies went to the radical Feda'iyan-e Islam, whose leader, Navvab Safavi, is shown here in a 1956 photograph. Safavi *(back row, center, with shaven head and beard)* was tried, sentenced, and executed for his role in assassination plots.

in 1953, called him "the learned philosopher, the discerning jurisconsult." Khomeini's lectures on ethics, which went on for eight years in the 1930s and 1940s, were "attended by hundreds of virtuous people from the centre itself and from other places," the historian wrote, and his lectures on theology were "better than any others." As a result, "much hope [was] now attached to him."

What finally brought Khomeini into the political spotlight were two events at the beginning of the 1960s: the introduction of a land-reform program by the shah, Muhammad Reza, (under pressure from the new U.S. administration of President John F. Kennedy) and the death of Borujerdi.

Landowners, afraid of losing their land, asked Borujerdi to declare the land-reform plan anti-Islamic (the concept of private property is included in shari'a). Since clerics, too, were concerned that they might lose some of the land that had been given to the religious community over the years, Borujerdi finally broke his silence on political matters and strongly protested.

In response, the shah deliberately insulted Borujerdi. Rather than visiting Borujerdi in his home, as was traditional, the shah had him taken to a shrine at the center of Qom. There Borujerdi was forced to wait for an hour. A further insult came when the shah finally arrived and merely said, "How are you, sir?" He then moved on, without waiting for a reply. For traditionalists like Khomeini, it was yet another anticlerical crime by the shah.

When Borujerdi died on March 30, 1961, Khomeini was not a candidate to replace him. Even though he was considered a marja' taqlid, at fifty-nine, he was still

Ayatollah Kashani's Opposition to British Rule

A column of British tanks arrives in Tehran.

Khomeini greatly admired Ayatollah Seyyed Abolqasem Kashani during this time. Born in 1882, Kashani had studied in Najaf, Iraq. He had opposed British rule over Iraq following World War I (1914–1918).

Kashani fled to Iran in 1921. He became a member of parliament in Tehran. He was also a member of the constituent assembly that voted to establish the Pahlavi dynasty in 1925.

After the Allied invasion, Kashani was arrested for his anti-British opinions. That made him a hero to the younger members of the clergy. When he was released in 1945, he became closely associated with the Feda'iyan-e Islam. Khomeini paid frequent visits to Kashani's home.

■ Shown here is one of Iran's enormous oil refineries at Abadan. Even with large oil revenues from a world economy needing oil, Iran asked the International Monetary Fund for economic assistance in the early 1960s.

thought to be too young. But the time was quickly approaching when he would put himself forward as a leader.

Economic Crisis and Reform

In the early 1960s, the Iranian government mismanaged the economy. It had a huge budget deficit and rising inflation. The shah worked with the International Monetary Fund to get a loan. The reforms the fund made to the economy plunged the country into a three-year-long recession.

Then elections to the Majles in July and August 1960 were found to be rigged. The government canceled the elections. The Iranian people were outraged. The elections were rescheduled for January 1961. When these, too, proved to be rigged, demonstrations rose up at Tehran University. More unrest followed in April. A massive street demonstration in support of a teachers' strike resulted in the fatal shooting of a teacher by police.

Under U.S. pressure, the shah dissolved the Majles in May 1961. He appointed Ali Amini as prime minister and gave him special powers for six months. Amini launched new economic cutbacks that further hurt Iranians. Worse, more land reforms

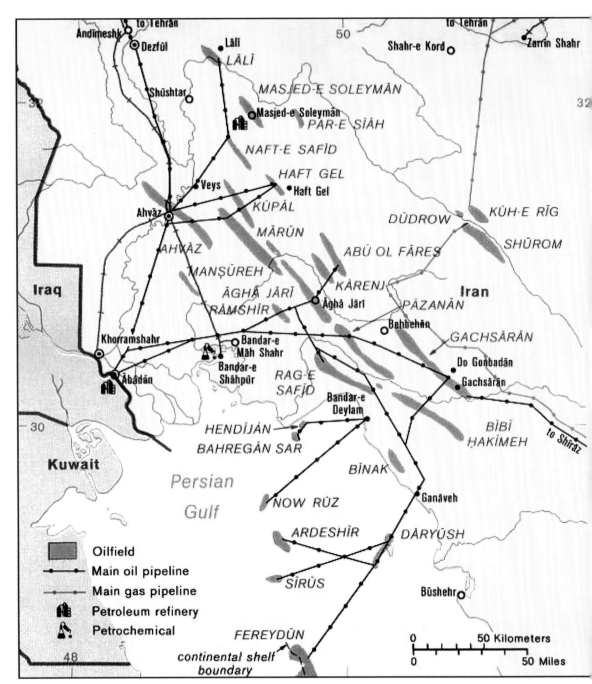

The Iranian oil reserves proved that the country could be an economic powerhouse. The shah's mismanagement of the government, however, squandered the wealth that could have helped his people. Ayatollahs in Iran were outraged for their followers' plight and began to openly criticize the government.

were put into place. These moves angered both ordinary citizens and the clergy. When Amini refused to hold free elections, he also lost the support of the National Front. Amini was forced to resign. On July 19, 1962, he was replaced by Asadollah Alam, a close friend of the shah's.

Khomeini Finally Acts

Khomeini did not publicly oppose the land-reform legislation. But a few weeks after Amini resigned, a new council election bill was announced. This bill allowed women to vote and did not require candidates to be Muslims. According to historian Hamid Ruhani-Ziyarati, Khomeini told a colleague that "the son of Reza Khan has embarked on the destruction of Islam in Iran. I will oppose this as long as the blood circulates in my veins." With Borujerdi dead, Khomeini no longer felt constrained to remain silent.

Khomeini met with the Ayatollahs Shariatmadari and Golpayegani. He hoped to establish a united front among Qom's leading clergymen. They couldn't agree on the wording of their protest, but they all sent separate public telegrams. When the shah didn't back down, Khomeini called a second meeting. This time he wrote to Prime Minister Alam. In the meantime, other groups were also protesting.

When the prime minister didn't reply, the ayatollahs sent another telegram to the shah. This telegram attacked Alam. The prime minister received a separate telegram. In it Khomeini accused him of wanting to abandon the Koran. In the face of mounting criticism, Alam agreed to allow only Muslims to stand as candidates or to vote. Oaths would be sworn on the Koran. Finally, the question of women voting would be put to the new parliament.

The unrest continued, however. In the end, the bill was abandoned and did not become law. The battle, however, had made Khomeini the regime's principal political opponent in the minds of most Iranians. He built on that, encouraging his Tehran supporters to frequently consult him. He told them to contact bazaar merchants, who feared that the shah's modernization efforts could diminish their power by creating new commercial and industrial competitors.

With Khomeini's help, the bazaar merchants established the Coalition of Islamic Societies. The coalition quickly established branches and contacts with other bazaar organizations across Iran. In effect, the coalition became an underground political party that was spreading Khomeini's ideas throughout the country. Likewise, the movement raised money for Khomeini. He passed this money on to theological centers, increasing his influence among them.

Fueling the Flames of Anger

The shah next announced a six-point bill called the White Revolution. It included land reform, the privatization of government factories, the right of women to vote and run in elections, the nationalization of natural resources, a literacy campaign, and a scheme for sharing industrial profits. A national referendum on the bill was to be held on January 26, 1963.

Khomeini urged the clergy to boycott the referendum as un-Islamic. At the same time, the secular opposition called for a boycott of the referendum as undemocratic. Three days before the vote was scheduled, the first of a series of demonstrations organized by

Khomeini's followers took place in Tehran. Riots and unrest followed over the next couple of days.

The shah visited Qom on January 24. At Khomeini's urging, people stayed home rather than welcome him. Shops and the school of theology were closed. Obviously angry, the shah viciously attacked the clergy in his speech. The government announced that the referendum was successful for the shah. The turnout was never revealed, however.

By now, Khomeini's opposition to the shah had made him famous. His photograph appeared in shops and homes. Pilgrims to Qom flocked to his house to hear his anti-shah sermons.

March 22, 1963, was the anniversary of the death of the sixth imam, Ja'far al-Sadiq, killed by the caliph, or monarch, of his time. Around the country, believers heard mullahs compare the shah to that murderous caliph. In Qom, the day's main event was to be held at the Feiziyeh School of Theology. Troops from the Imperial Guard were deployed around it, and the service itself, disrupted by secret police agents, turned into a riot. A security agent and three seminarians were killed (security forces threw the students off the roof). Many others were seriously injured.

Over the next few weeks, the government boosted its own propaganda efforts. It claimed the riots had been between peasants who supported the land reform and clerics and students who opposed it. Khomeini's statements were also circulated around the country. The shah tried to discredit him by attacking his views as backward and not good for the country. When that didn't work, the shah threatened him. Khomeini continued to speak out.

Ayatollah Khomeini

■ The Iranian city of Qom became a center of religious learning in 1921. Forty-two years later, Khomeini based his political opposition to the shah's government in Qom, ninety miles south of Tehran.

The month of Moharram, in the Islamic calendar, is a time for flagellation (whipping one's self), chest-beating, and weeping. Khomeini promised to return to Feiziyeh on June 3, known as Ashura, to deliver a speech that would shake the regime. Speaking to a huge demonstration organized by his students, he insulted the shah in a way no one had ever before dared to do in public, calling him a "wretched, miserable man." That same day in Tehran, an estimated 100,000 people marched outside the shah's Marble Palace, shouting "Death to the dictator!" and "God save you, Khomeini!"

Two days later, on June 5, 1963, Khomeini was arrested.

CHAPTER FOUR
THE AYATOLLAH IN EXILE

■ The Iranian government placed Khomeini under house arrest in 1963. Here, he sits waiting to meet with supporters. After his arrest and confinement, Khomeini began to attack the government with words more than ever.

K homeini's arrest took place at dawn in his son Mostafa's house. When the public learned of the arrest, riots began in the streets. They quickly turned bloody. Crowds attacked government offices all over

Iran. Many Khomeini supporters were arrested. The government declared martial law (military rule). It put tanks and soldiers onto the streets, with orders to shoot to kill. Several hundred people died as rioting continued.

Some people in the government wanted to execute Khomeini. Others felt that killing him would make the situation worse. Eventually, he was put under house arrest in a Tehran suburb. For one day, he was "free" to meet people. The number of people who came to see him alarmed the government, which quickly sealed the area off to visitors.

The shah continued his propaganda campaign. He called the clergy enemies of modernization. To fight them, he turned loose the Savak—his secret police. The Savak harassed, searched, and interrogated clerics and seminary students. They thought this would stop the spread of anti-shah statements.

On March 8, 1964, the shah appointed a new prime minister, Hassan Ali Mansur. Mansur thought the shah's anticlerical campaign had been so successful it was safe to let Khomeini return to Qom. On April 7, 1964, ten months after being arrested, Khomeini was driven home.

All of Qom celebrated Khomeini's return. Thousands flocked to his home. Khomeini immediately resumed his attacks on the shah. He shifted his focus from strictly religious concerns to questions of sovereignty, economic health, and social justice. This was his way to reach out to the secular dissidents as well as the clerical ones.

Along came a new outrage: a law giving diplomatic immunity to American military personnel. This law meant that military people couldn't be tried by Iranian courts, no matter what laws they broke. Khomeini accused the government of high treason for turning Iranian sovereignty over to America.

Arrest and Exile

For the government, this was the last straw. Khomeini was arrested again on the morning of November 4, 1964. By evening he was being flown into exile by a military transport plane on its way to Ankara, Turkey. After a few days in a hotel, Khomeini was sent to Bursa, Turkey. There he lived for three months with the family of Colonel Ali Cetiner of Turkish military intelligence. After that he was moved to other houses, but the Cetiners continued to be his hosts. On January 3, 1965, Khomeini's son, Mostafa, joined him in exile.

At first Khomeini was angry at the Cetiners' secular lifestyle (he yelled at Ali's wife, Melahat, and twelve-year-old daughter, Payan, for not covering their heads). Soon, though, he learned to adapt. Ali Bey Cetiner published a memoir of the family's recollections of Khomeini's stay with them in the newspaper *Melliyat* in 1987. In those memoirs, Melahat recalled, "He told us that throughout his life he had never stood up for a woman. But he would stand up when I entered the room. He had also never looked a woman in the face. Later, he began to look me in the face as well. He would chat to me amicably and smile." In fact, she said, "He was a nice old man and very polite."

In all, Khomeini spent eleven months with the Cetiners. He never discussed politics, but his followers in Iran had certainly not forgotten him; they sent him so much money that in less than a year, he was a millionaire.

Back in Iran, Khomeini's supporters kept pressuring the shah to end Khomeini's exile. International human

■ While in exile in France, Ayatollah Khomeini met with followers eager to learn how they could help their countrymen back in Iran. Khomeini found that exile was a better way to spread his message because the West was open and tolerant of subversive views.

rights organizations and the United Nations also called for him to be allowed to return. In October 1965, he was allowed to leave Turkey, but he was not allowed to go to Iran. Instead, he was sent to the holy Shiite city of Najaf in Iraq. Both he and Melahat Cetiner cried when they parted at the Ankara airport.

Life in Iraq

Khomeini did not see eye-to-eye with Najaf's religious leadership. He called the city a "den of snakes."

In Iraq, the Shiite clergy had traditionally maintained a live-and-let-live attitude toward the Iraqi government. As a result, Khomeini could not muster the same influence in Iraq that he could in Iran. In a letter to a student, he wrote, "I do not know what sin I have committed to be confined to Najaf in the few remaining days of my life."

The closest Khomeini came to becoming involved in Iraqi politics was to help keep students at the theological school in Najaf. They had been persecuted by the government and were not given any money for schooling. Khomeini boosted their monthly stipends out of his own funds. He first increased the stipends from two dinars to three dinars a month (at the current exchange rate, U.S. $6.43–$9.65). By the time Khomeini left Iraq, he was paying students fifty dinars ($160.82) a month.

Khomeini continued to be heavily involved in Iranian politics. His ongoing sermons and statements were copied or taped and smuggled into Iran. Khomeini's influence began to grow among Iranian student organizations.

■ While living in France, Khomeini meets with students to talk about Iranian politics. Wealthy Iranian families sent their children to Western universities. Khomeini used these students to create a fervor over the Iranian government's suppression of its people back home.

Ayatollah Hakim, who had taken Ayatollah Borujerdi's position as marja', died in 1970. Khomeini did not feel he could accept any of the contenders as undisputed leader of the Shiite community. But he also felt that he could not campaign for the position. Ayatollah Kho'i, based in Najaf, was eventually recognized as marja'.

Political Influence from Abroad

In a series of lectures in the early 1970s, Khomeini set out his view of how an Islamic state should be governed and established. The lectures were collected, translated into English by Hamid Algar, and published in 1981 as *Islam and Revolution: Writings and Declarations.* Khomeini's plan for overthrowing the shah boiled down to four points: "(i) severing all relations with governmental institutions; (ii) refusing to cooperate with them; (iii) refraining from any action that might be construed as aiding them; and (iv) creating new judicial, financial, economic, cultural and political institutions."

The most important element of his theory of governing was the *velayat-e faqih*, "the governance of the jurist." In mainstream Shiite thinking, the authority of the jurist, or *faqih*, is limited to being the guardian of widows and orphans. But Khomeini made the faqih central.

An Islamic state conforms only to God's law, Khomeini said. So there is no need for legislators. All an Islamic state needs is a planning committee that sets up government structures in accordance with God's law. The faqih's role is to ensure that everything the planning committee comes up with adheres to Islamic law. Anything that does not is done away with.

■ Khomeini gained political influence at home from his lectures and writings made while abroad. His shrewd political moves forced the shah to crack down against the ayatollah's followers. This would prove to be the shah's eventual undoing.

This was a radical notion to orthodox Shiite leaders. In fact, Ayatollah Kho'i argued strongly against Khomeini's position right up until the revolution.

Working Against the Shah

Meanwhile, Khomeini's Iranian followers were not meekly hiding away. The Coalition of Islamic Societies added an armed wing (a small group with guns) shortly after Khomeini went into exile. They made a list of people to assassinate, including the shah. Two months after Khomeini went to Turkey, the coalition succeeded in assassinating Prime Minister Mansur. However, the assassin was caught. Many members of the coalition were imprisoned and four were executed.

A more successful coalition tactic was the establishment of private Islamic primary and secondary schools for boys and girls. These schools offset the shah's influence and even introduced Khomeini's ideas of the ideal Islamic state into textbooks.

Iran was in good economic shape during the late 1960s and early 1970s because of huge oil revenues. The shah, however, had made his government more repressive. The Savak were everywhere, looking for dissidents and arresting people. Everyone knew the elections to the Majles every four years were rigged. Much of the shah's power was based on an alliance with the United States. Many considered this colonialism. The modern secular lifestyle in the cities struck traditional Muslims as wicked.

Throughout the 1970s, a communist guerrilla group called the Feda'iyan-e Khalq ("warriors of the people") staged many attacks. Another radical religious group called the Mojahedin-e Khalq-e Iran ("the holy warriors of the

■ Midday prayers at the Shah Mosque in Tehran (now called the Imam Khomeini Mosque) brings the faithful from their jobs to offer prayers to Allah. Khomeini's political strength grew from those faithful to Islam who saw the shah as a despot.

Iranian people") also fought against the shah's government. It split in 1975 into communist and religious factions.

Khomeini did not back any of the various secular groups opposing the shah. "I despise these treacherous grouplets, whether communist or Marxist, or deviant from the Shi'ite faith under whatever name or title, and I consider them traitors to the country, to Islam and Shi'ism," he wrote in a letter to Morteza Motahari, one of his leading supporters and aides in Iran.

Nevertheless, these and other "grouplets" helped make university students more radical in the 1970s, priming them for the coming revolution.

The Final Insult to the Iranian People

In March 1975, the shah decided to make Iran a one-party state. He required all adults to join the new Rastakhiz (Resurgence) Party. For the first time, people felt that they were being publicly forced to support the regime, no matter how they really felt. In 1976, the government launched a populist campaign against over-pricing that turned the business community against it. And to top it off, the shah threw out the Islamic calendar and put in place a new one that began with the establishment of the Persian Empire, instantly changing the date from 1355 to 2535.

Khomeini forbade the faithful from joining the party or using the new calendar. In June 1976, on the thirteenth anniversary of the 1963 uprising, pro-Khomeini groups staged a major demonstration in Qom. It was put down violently by the government. More guerrilla groups sprang up, many with links to the Coalition of Islamic Societies.

Street protests against the shah's rule turned violent during the late 1970s in Tehran. Here, protesters are trying to break into a building next door to a prison in order to release the prisoners.

In 1976, with Khomeini's permission, a new organization called the Society of Militant Clergy was formed. Its various branches organized debates, strikes, and demonstrations. It also recruited young men and, most important, distributed Khomeini's statements.

Then, in 1977, the economic boom ended in Iran. The United States elected a new president, Jimmy Carter, who had made human rights a key part of his policy. Hoping his administration would support them, supporters of Dr. Mosaddeq sent an open letter to the shah urging him to

■ During Shah Muhammad Reza Pahlavi's crackdown of dissidents in 1977, he met with United States president Jimmy Carter. The Iranian protesters viewed the United States as the enemy of the Iranian people for supporting the shah.

improve the country's human rights situation and establish a more democratic government.

The shah responded by replacing Prime Minister Amir Abbas Hoveida with Jamshid Amuzegar, the general secretary of the Rastakhiz Party. The change was cosmetic, but it gave hope to the dissidents, and the call for human rights grew stronger.

Late in 1977, a personal tragedy suddenly thrust Khomeini into the media spotlight. On October 23, Khomeini's son, Mostafa, died suddenly. Although the cause appeared to be a heart attack, many people thought he might have been murdered by the Savak. A major service at a central Tehran mosque heaped praise on Khomeini and Mostafa. In Qom, demonstrators called for Khomeini's return.

More demonstrations broke out, both in the United States and in Iran, when the shah visited Washington, D.C., on November 15. But when President Carter paid a return visit to Tehran on New Year's Eve, he toasted the shah with champagne, declared himself a "close personal friend," and referred to the "respect, admiration and love" of the shah's people for

■ One of the more violent factions of Iranian protesters was made up of students from Tehran University. Shown here is one of the daily protests in January 1979. An estimated 400,000 protesters gathered at the university on this day.

their ruler. To the Iranian dissidents, it was a signal they could expect no support from Washington.

Days later, the proverbial straw finally broke the camel's back. An article in the afternoon daily *Ettela'at*, entitled "Black and Red Imperialism," personally insulted Khomeini. People in Qom poured into the streets, shouting "Long live Khomeini!" and "Death to Pahlavi rule!" Even clerics who didn't normally support Khomeini felt compelled to defend him. Six demonstrators were killed. Further demonstrations occurred around the country, coinciding with the Muslim cycle of mourning on the seventh and fortieth day after a death.

Overthrowing the Shah

The shah appointed yet another new prime minister, Ja'far Sharif Emami. He abolished the imperial calendar and declared that all political parties had a right to be active, but it was too late.

On September 6, 1977, thousands demonstrated in Tehran. For the first time, they called for "Islamic rule." The shah banned further marches. Nevertheless, half a million people took to the streets on September 7. On September 8, a smaller crowd gathered. Martial law was declared. Many demonstrators were arrested, and others were shot and killed.

Unbeknownst to the demonstrators, the shah had cancer and his health was failing. He sought advice from the British, American, and even Soviet ambassadors. He tried to pressure Iraq to restrict Khomeini's activity. Khomeini had already decided to leave Najaf, however. Turned back at the border to Kuwait, he instead flew to Paris, arriving there with his son, Ahmad, and a few friends on October 12.

Khomeini intended to stay in France only until he could find an Islamic country to go to. However, he soon found advantages to being in France. Foreign journalists flocked to the village outside Paris where he was settled in a small villa. He became a media celebrity. The CBS news program *60 Minutes* interviewed him. Khomeini made daily speeches and led daily prayers that drew large crowds. His statements were transmitted by telephone to

$\text{A}_{\text{yatollah}}$ $\text{K}_{\text{homeini}}$

■ Ayatollah Khomeini is shown having one of his many meetings with Iranian students at his home in Pontchartrain, France, in November 1978. Within a month, protests in Iran would draw nearly 3 million people demanding the shah's removal.

Iran, where they were taped, transcribed, photocopied, and distributed.

Three men always at Khomeini's side in France, Abol-Hasan Bani-Sadr, Ebrahim Yazdi, and Sadeq Qotbzadeh, translated his statements to the Western media and translated the Western media's reports for Khomeini. Partly through their efforts, the West believed Khomeini envisioned something like a democratic state in Iran (they seemed to have believed it themselves). He didn't discuss his idea of velayat-e faqih. He even suggested that a woman might someday become president.

Iranian intellectuals who feared that Khomeini's Islamic state was incompatible with their own hopes for a freer, more modern society had little choice but to at least superficially support him, because the only other choice was to support the shah.

The shah's situation grew worse. His security forces were spread too thin to keep order. Demonstrations spread out of control everywhere. In November the shah installed a new military government under General Ghulam-Reza Azhari.

But on December 10 and 11, 1978, up to 17 million people nationwide—

The Three Wise Men

Khomeini's three main aides in France all eventually fell out of favor.

Abol-Hasan Bani-Sadr had moved to Paris in the early 1960s. There he wrote extensively on Iranian politics, attacking the shah's regime. He met Khomeini in 1972 in Iraq and became an admirer. He made all the preparations for Khomeini's move to Paris. Bani-Sadr became the first president of the new Islamic Republic of Iran but was driven from government in 1981 and fled back to Paris.

Before joining Khomeini in Paris, Dr. Ebrahim Yazdi spent several years in Texas, preaching against the shah's regime to Islamic students while earning a doctorate in genetics. He served as the new Iranian government's foreign minister but resigned after the seizure of the U.S. Embassy.

Dr. Yazdi went on to become leader of the liberal Freedom Movement of Iran. In 1997 he was arrested for speaking against the leader, but he was later released. In 2001, he went to the United States for medical treatment. While he was there, he was charged in Iran with plotting to overthrow the government and was sentenced to death. He nonetheless returned to Iran in 2002. He died in February 2003.

Sadeq Qotbzadeh was an anti-shah student activist who moved to France after he was expelled from the United States in 1969. After the revolution, he became the head of radio and television in Iran and was eventually made foreign minister. He resigned in 1980 and was executed in 1982 for allegedly plotting to overthrow Khomeini.

2 to 3 million in Tehran alone—marched peacefully. They demanded the removal of the shah and the return of Khomeini.

The shah kept struggling. He set up yet another new government, this time headed by opposition leader Dr. Shahpur Bakhtiar, but it wasn't enough. On January 16, 1979, he left Iran. He never went back.

On February 1, 1979, Ayatollah Khomeini returned to Iran.

CHAPTER FIVE

THE IMAM

■ Khomeini's return home to Tehran in February 1979, signaled a new era for the oppressed people of Iran. Khomeini had spent fifteen years in exile.

Khomeini's plane landed at 9:30 AM in Tehran. A welcoming committee set up by the Islamic Revolutionary Council met him. (Khomeini had proclaimed the creation of this council on January 13. Its purpose was to establish a transitional government to replace the Bakhtiar government.)

Among the chants that greeted Khomeini was "Khomeini, O Imam." In Muslim countries "imam" is a term applied to a leader or prayer leader. In Shiite Iran, however, the title had always been reserved for one of the twelve infallible leaders of the early Shia. The implications were obvious. To his supporters, Khomeini was more than an ordinary man.

Setting Up a New Government

Khomeini set up temporary headquarters at Refah School. This was a girls' high school close to the parliament building. His first task was to appoint a provisional prime minister. He and the Islamic Revolutionary Council chose Mehdi Bazargan. Bazargan was a leader of the Freedom Movement of Iran, an Islamic modernist and democrat. He was charged with holding a referendum on changing the country's political system to an Islamic republic. That would lead to the election of a Constituent Assembly. The assembly would ratify a new constitution and elect delegates for a new parliament.

But at the February 5, 1979, news conference at which he announced Bazargan's appointment, Khomeini issued a decree that set the tone for Iran's future. "This is not an ordinary government," he said. "It is a government based on the shari'a. Opposing this government means opposing the shari'a of Islam . . . Revolt against God's government is a revolt against God. Revolt against God is blasphemy."

Dr. Bakhtiar's shah-appointed government began to crumble as members of parliament and government

Ayatollah Khomeini

■ Upon his return to Tehran, Khomeini set up offices to direct the establishment of a new government. Here he addresses his followers at a mosque near his home in the city.

officials resigned. There was fear of a military coup (overthrow of the government). The Americans used their influence within the military to help avert it.

On February 8, hundreds of air force technicians came to Rafeh School to pledge their support for Khomeini. The Imperial Guard's most elite unit, the Immortals, attacked several air force bases later that day in response. Guerrillas from the Feda'iyan and Mojahedin rushed to the bases. Fighting spread throughout Tehran. Police stations and army barracks were attacked.

Bakhtiar announced a curfew, but Khomeini told his supporters to ignore it. He threatened a *jihad*, or holy war, against any army units that didn't surrender. Guerrilla units attacked the Immortals' barracks. They also took over American military buildings and seized the television and radio station and other government offices.

On the morning of February 11, the Supreme Military Council gave in to the inevitable and declared that the military would remain neutral. It meant that Khomeini had won. But the rioting and fighting threatened to

Ayatollah Khomeini

■ Khomeini's control over the Iranian government came quickly. He accepted the greetings of his followers, such as these shown here, then threatened the military with a holy war if they did not remain neutral. Once the military backed down, Khomeini reigned supreme.

spread out of control. Bazargan and Khomeini urged the population to refrain from looting and taking revenge on the shah's officials. But the pressure for vengeance was so great that Khomeini eventually agreed to a series of summary trials and executions. Four leading generals, including the former chief of the Savak, General Nassiri, were shot on the roof of Refah School. Executions continued for weeks, despite protests from moderates and the international community.

Meanwhile, the various groups that accepted Khomeini's leadership had banded together to form the Islamic Republican Party (IRP). Its goal was to make sure the clergy wielded supreme power in the government. Its "muscle" was provided by the Hezbollah ("Party of God"). Hezbollah members attacked demonstrators, the offices of opposition groups, and newspapers.

The Islamic Revolutionary Guards Corps was also formed. It was to "protect the revolution from destructive forces and counter-revolutionaries," says Khomeini biographer Baqer Moin. By the end of 1979, it boasted 25,000 men.

Khomeini Takes Full Control

In March 1979, Khomeini returned to his home in Qom for the first time in fifteen years. The focus of all government decision-making shifted with him. He had endless meetings with politicians and gave almost daily public audiences, often broadcast live on radio or television.

On March 30 and 31, the promised referendum was held. Ninety-seven percent of the electorate voted yes to an Islamic republic, even though nobody knew exactly what sort of government that was.

They soon found out. With the referendum over, Khomeini began issuing decrees and orders without consulting his chosen prime minister. For instance, he ordered that all female government employees in Tehran should wear traditional Islamic dress. The power of the Islamic Revolutionary Council grew to the point where, led by Khomeini, it held all the real power. Bazargan's supposed official government was as helpless as Bakhtiar's had been.

Various groups took note and took action. In April and May, a series of assassinations by an anti-clerical Islamist group called Forqan killed several of Khomeini's supporters. One such assassination was of Morteza Motahari, who had been Khomeini's right-hand man in Iran during his exile. Khomeini wept openly during Motahari's service of remembrance. Even some leading clerics denounced the IRP and the revolutionary courts.

In the midst of all this, the shape of a new constitution was being debated. A very liberal draft constitution had been written in Paris and approved by Khomeini. Now, however, that draft was unacceptable to him. He found that it did not embrace his concept of the velayat-e faqih.

Bazargan wanted to have an elected Constituent Assembly with nearly 300 members designing the constitution. But Khomeini overruled him. He announced that a much smaller Assembly of Experts with only seventy members would undertake the task. The smaller number made it easier for the Islamic Revolutionary Council to rig the results, producing a council dominated by clergy loyal to Khomeini.

Khomeini and the IRP continued to attack liberal and left-wing groups, especially the National Democratic

■ Khomeini was seventy-six years old when he became the leader of
Iran. Nearly his entire life had been in the service of Islamic studies and
teaching. Now he was attempting to transfer that knowledge into
Islamic rule of a national government structure. Many Iranian intellectuals feared that this would hurt Iran's ability to modernize.

Front of Iran, whose demonstrations were well-attended, despite regular attacks by Hezbollah.

On August 9, three days before the Assembly of Experts began discussing the constitution, the National Front held a demonstration to protest the closing of *Ayandegan*, a daily newspaper. Once again Hezbollah attacked.

Just a year before, biographer Baqer Moin notes, Khomeini had told a Western journalist that an Islamic republic "is a democratic state in the true sense of the word . . . everyone . . . can voice their own opinion." But the day after the demonstration, the revolutionary prosecutor of Tehran issued a warrant for the arrest of one of the front's leaders. Included in the order was the closing of twenty-six major newspapers and magazines. It seemed that neither peaceful protest nor freedom of the press would be permitted in the new Islamic republic.

America: "The Great Satan"

On October 22, 1979, the shah was admitted into the United States for cancer treatment. Khomeini saw that as evidence of American plotting. He began to refer to America as "the Great Satan."

On November 1, Prime Minister Bazargan, while in Algeria for celebrations marking the anniversary of the Algerian Revolution, was photographed shaking hands with President Carter's national security adviser, Zbigniew Brzezinski. In the Iranian press, Bazargan was accused of coming under U.S. influence.

Then, on November 4, 1979, radical students occupied the U.S. Embassy in Tehran and took ninety hostages.

■ Khomeini allowed Iranian students to capture and hold American hostages, despite protests from Iranian prime minister Bazargan. Khomeini decided that the students deserved this symbolic act against "the Great Satan," America.

■ Protesters against foreign intervention in Iranian politics took pleasure in gathering outside the U.S. Embassy in Tehran. This photo shows the protesters praying at the embassy gates while, inside, students held hostages at gunpoint.

Women and African American marine guards were soon released. Fifty-two diplomats were held in places all over Tehran. The crisis dragged on for 444 days. It ended on January 20, 1981, after Ronald Reagan took over as U.S. president from Jimmy Carter. A failed attempt by the U.S. military to rescue the hostages, in April 1980, further humiliated the United States.

Bazargan wanted to remove the students immediately. Khomeini and the Islamic Revolutionary Council refused to support him. He and his government resigned.

Bazargan's departure, coupled with the new constitution, dimmed the hopes of democratic reformers.

The New Iranian Constitution

The new Iranian constitution named God the nation's sovereign. His vice regent was the *valiy-e faqih*, the leader, Khomeini. He could declare war. He could appoint military leaders. It was up to him to confirm the president and choose the highest-ranking judicial officials. He or his representatives, the clergy, could also veto almost any decision made at any other level of the government.

A referendum on the new constitution was scheduled for December 3. Khomeini used the hostage crisis to defuse the widespread opposition to it. Although he hadn't said much about it at first, he now came out in full support of the student's actions. He painted those who opposed the constitution as being supporters of America. He also gained support from left-wing organizations that applauded his standing up to the United States. The crisis lifted Khomeini to new heights of international recognition.

The December referendum massively endorsed the new constitution. But many opposition groups boycotted the referendum. Early in 1980, Abol-Hasan Bani-Sadr, who had been at Khomeini's side in France, was elected Iran's first president. But he soon found himself in difficulty. The IRP worked against him, and Khomeini put a powerful ayatollah in place as chief justice of the Supreme Court.

Bani-Sadr's troubles worsened when the IRP ended up dominating the first Islamic Parliament, elected in May. The IRP refused to accept any of the candidates Bani-Sadr put forward as prime minister, finally forcing

Bani-Sadr to accept the IRP's candidate, Mohammad Ali Raja'i. Raja'i was a longtime Khomeini supporter whom Bani-Sadr considered incompetent. As well, the IRP took control of every government department.

The Iran–Iraq War and Internal Rebellion

Khomeini had made Bani-Sadr commander in chief of the armed forces. In September 1980, Iraq, led by Saddam Hussein, invaded Iran. The Iraqi army swiftly captured Khorramshahr, Iran's largest port, and the center of Iran's oil industry.

Khomeini knew Iran's defenses were in poor shape, but he refused to compromise with Saddam Hussein. Khomeini considered Hussein, a non-religious leader of an Islamic country, an infidel. Instead, Khomeini called on the Shiite population of Iraq to overthrow Hussein.

Bani-Sadr found he was more welcome near the front lines than he was in Tehran. Therefore, he spent nearly all his time in southern Iran. He had become the best hope for reform of all the opposition groups, especially the Mojahedin. A Mojahedin demonstration in Tehran on April 27, 1981, drew 150,000 people. The chief prosecutor responded by banning the Mojahedin from demonstrating, a blow to Bani-Sadr.

Then, on June 8, 1981, Bani-Sadr called for "resistance to dictatorship" in a speech at the Shirza air force base. That was seen as advocating the overthrow of the government. On June 10, Khomeini stripped Bani-Sadr of the title of commander in chief. The Majles moved to impeach him. On June 20, the Mojahedin, supported by most opposition groups, called for a mass march against dictatorship, the most direct challenge to

Khomeini's leadership so far. Tens of thousands marched, around twenty people were killed, and hundreds more were arrested.

On June 21, the Majles voted to impeach Bani-Sadr. The next day Khomeini dismissed him. Bani-Sadr went into hiding and called for a mass uprising. A week of fighting followed. More than fifty opponents to the religious leadership were killed.

On June 28, a bomb destroyed the IRP headquarters in southern Tehran. The blast killed more than seventy people who were meeting there, including cabinet ministers, nearly two dozen members of parliament, and Ayatollah Beheshti, one of Khomeini's most important supporters. Khomeini blamed the Mojahedin, and the government launched an all-out assault on the group and other Khomeini opponents. Within days, Bani-Sadr fled in an air force plane to Paris, where he continued to criticize the Iranian government and plot his return until he was assassinated.

By late August, 900 government opponents had been executed. By the end of 1981, according to the human-rights organization Amnesty International, the number reached 2,500.

A popular new president, Mohammad Ali Raja'i, elected in July, was killed by a bomb on August 30, along with his prime minister, Mohammad Javad Bahonar. His murder resulted in immense public anger toward the Mojahedin.

Tyranny Takes Over Iran

In an effort to stamp out opposition, Khomeini announced that it was the religious duty of all individuals to keep

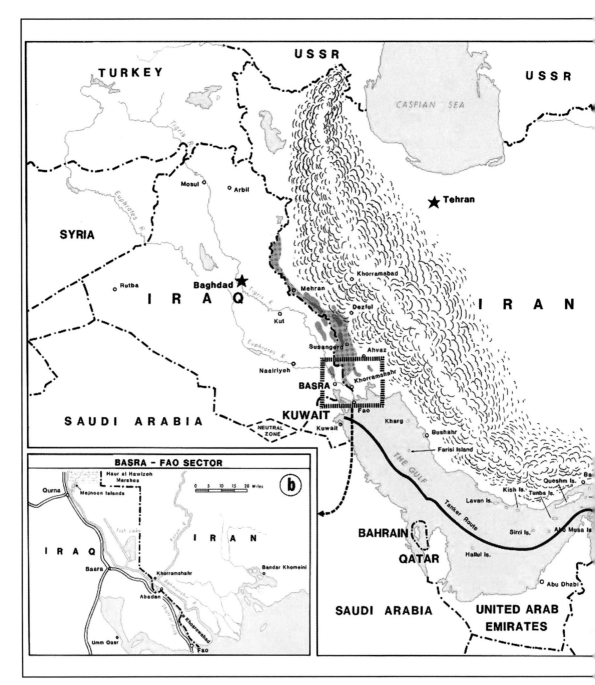

■ The Iran-Iraq War lasted eight years and killed more than a million people. Iraqi president Saddam Hussein ordered an invasion of Iran. He used the disputed water rights along the Shatt al Arab River bordering the two countries as his excuse.

watch on their neighbors. The result was a reign of terror. Friends and family members turned each other in for trial and execution. Executions led to more assassinations, which led to more executions. Thousands died.

The bloodletting convinced Khomeini that he needed more, not fewer, clergy involved in running the state. The country's third president, Ali Khamene'i, who took over on October 20, was a clergyman and a personal favorite of Khomeini's.

With internal opposition at least temporarily repressed, the Iranian government gave more attention to the continuing war with Iraq. Iran launched new offensives in the autumn of 1981. A series of victories over the next few months freed the country's oil centers and culminated in the recapture of Khorramshahr in May 1982.

At that point, Iraq seemed to be willing to negotiate an end to the war. Saddam Hussein had said he wanted to send his troops to fight the Israelis, who had invaded Lebanon after Iraqi agents severely wounded its ambassador in London. Khomeini instead chose to launch fresh offensives. He had come to see the war as "God's

■ Both the Iranian and Iraqi militaries suffered humiliating defeats on the battlefield. Huge scores of men were taken prisoner on both sides and had to wait out the end of the war for many years. Shown here are Iraqi prisoners taking part in prayers during a Friday in Tehran.

hidden gift." By this he meant that it was a means to ensure the survival of the clergy and enable them to build the Islamic society he envisioned. He had also come to believe that he needed to export his revolution outside Iran if it were to survive. He saw himself as the liberator of all oppressed Muslims. As his son, Ahmad, later wrote in his memoirs, "For eight years our news was headline news throughout the world. Every missile we sent to Iraq carried with it the Imam's thoughts to the world. It was the Imam's line of communication to every

Hojjat al-Islam Ali Khamene'i

Ali Khamene'i casts his ballot during Iran's first elections since the revolution.

Ali Khamene'i's family came from Azerbaijan, but he was raised in Mashhad, Iran. During the 1960s and 1970s, his opposition to the shah landed him in jail and internal exile. As a respected scholar, he wrote and translated many books.

Khamene'i served as Khomeini's special representative in the Supreme Defense Council. He was later made deputy defense minister and then was put in charge of the Revolutionary Guards. He survived the June 1981 bombing with a crippled arm and became general secretary of the Islamic Republican Party.

He served two terms as president. After Khomeini's death, he was appointed as the new valiy-e faqih, a post he continues to hold to this day.

single Muslim." That being the case, Khomeini pursued the war without regard for the cost. Over eight years, the war killed between 180,000 and 300,000 Iranians and cost at least $300 billion.

As the war ground on, Khomeini consolidated his position among the clergy. In the spring of 1982, a plot to assassinate Khomeini was uncovered. It involved the former foreign minister Sadeq Qotbzadeh, another of the three men who had been at Khomeini's side in France. Qotbzadeh and as many as seventy army officers convicted of being his coconspirators were executed.

Qotbzadeh confessed that Ayatollah Shariatmadari, the spiritual leader of the Mojahedin, had approved the plan. Khomeini forced Shariatmadari to make a public confession and plead for forgiveness. Then he had Shariatmadari "defrocked," forced to abandon his religious clothing.

Within the customs of Shiite Islam, the defrocking of a marja' recognized as treacherous by his followers, and not by any outside body, is technically meaningless. Only the marja's followers can remove him

■ Although opposition to the war caused social and political unrest at home, many soldiers on the battlefield saw fighting as their duty to their ayatollah and Islam. Here, fighters have pasted images of Khomeini on their antiaircraft guns to honor their leader during battle.

from his position. But it humiliated Shariatmadari and silenced other senior clergymen who realized their high position offered no protection from Khomeini if they dared oppose him.

Trying to Force Normalcy

On December 15, 1982, Khomeini felt secure enough to decree that in the future, the courts must ensure that people's rights and the due process of Islamic law were protected. The decree signaled to the middle class that something approaching normalcy might be returning.

Eliminating nonclerical parties from the political process didn't end conflicts. The clergy had its own factions. In the Majles elected in 1984, the majority of members belonged to reformist and radical factions. That put them at odds with the highly conservative Council of Guardians. This was the committee that had to examine legislation to ensure it was compatible with both the shari'a and the constitution. The result was near-paralysis in both the government and the economy, as the Council of Guardians usually refused proposals from the Majles for a more active role in the government.

Khomeini seems not to have taken a side. He was usually willing to allow the clergy to debate issues, and he only occasionally made rulings to settle otherwise thorny debates. (For example, traditionalists wanted to ban all music, and radicals were broadcasting it; Khomeini decreed that as long as music is edifying and enhances revolutionary and Islamic feelings, it would not be forbidden.)

However, Khomeini was more than willing to take action when he felt it necessary. In January 1987, Khomeini authorized the government to punish hoarders without going to court. Later he introduced a bill cutting off essential services from companies that failed to pay their taxes or their employees' insurance, or to observe the laws that protected workers. The Council of Guardians challenged him.

Khomeini's resulting decree was historic. In a public exchange of letters with the council, he wrote that the Islamic government of Iran is the continuation of prophecy and Islamic rule pioneered by the Prophet. A few months later he made his meaning more explicit. "Islamic government," he wrote in response to a sermon delivered by President Ali Khamene'i on January 1, 1988, at Tehran University, "is one of the primary injunctions in Islam." Not only that, he went on, but it takes "precedence over all subsidiary precepts, even praying, fasting, and performing the Hajj [the pilgrimage to Mecca]."

In an effort to break the logjam between the parliament and the Council of Guardians, Khomeini set up a new thirteen-man Council for Assessing the Interests of the System. Since there was no provision in the constitution for such a body, many people saw it as proof that Khomeini had become an absolute dictator.

Khomeini saw himself as a liberator. In 1987, he sent a message to participants of the hajj. It called on the Muslims there to demonstrate against "pagans," such as the Soviet Union, the United States, and Israel, and their "servants," the Arab kings (this included the rulers of Saudi Arabia, where Mecca is located). After receiving the message, Iranian pilgrims in Mecca rushed toward the Great Mosque, intending to take it over. The Saudi authorities panicked and fired into the crowd. Nearly 400 people were killed.

Resolution to War

By the beginning of 1988, the Iran-Iraq War was taking a serious toll on Iran. That spring, Iraqi Scud missiles bombarded Tehran. Iranian troops were driven back by the Iraqis, who used chemical weapons on their enemy. The U.S. Navy blew up two Iranian oil rigs and two Iranian vessels in the Persian Gulf. Khomeini's opponents in Iran became more vocal than they had been in years.

Then on July 3, 1988, an American warship shot down a commercial Iran Air jet, which the warship claimed it mistook for an attacking aircraft. The shooting killed 290 civilians. The Iranian government felt the country could take no more disasters. Concerned that his revolution could be in danger of collapse, Khomeini agreed to accept a negotiated end to the war.

On July 18, Iran announced it would unconditionally accept a United Nations Security Council resolution of a year before aimed at ending the hostilities. Khomeini called his agreement to the resolution "more bitter than poison." His son, Ahmad, recalled in his memoirs, "After accepting the cease-fire he could no longer walk. He kept

■ The Iran-Iraq War stopped only when foreign governments finally intervened. When the USS *Vincennes* shot down an Iran Air commercial jet, mourners took to the streets with coffins during a mass funeral. Other protesters demanded that the war finally be stopped.

saying, 'My Lord, I submit to your will.' He never again spoke in public . . . [eventually] he fell ill and was taken to the hospital."

Khomeini had had heart problems since his time in Iraq, but they had gotten worse in the early 1980s. He also had cancer, and his eyesight was failing.

A Crumbling Revolution?

In the late summer and early autumn of 1988, Khomeini set up a three-man commission and ordered it to take firm action against all political prisoners. The move was in response to a brief military fight by the Mojahedin from its base in Iraq. Over the next two months, several thousand prisoners were executed for failing to renounce their past beliefs. In some cases, they had originally been imprisoned for nothing more than handing out leaflets.

The purge of the prisons led to a crisis in the delicate matter of who would succeed Khomeini after his death. In 1985, an Assembly of Experts, after two years of deliberation, had chosen Ayatollah Hussein Ali Montazeri as that successor. A firm believer in the Islamic revolution, he also railed against corruption, injustice, and bureaucratic bungling. He was also more willing to tolerate moderate opposition leaders than Khomeini. Montazeri let it be known that he thought the violent purging of the prisons was anti-Islamic.

In early 1989, Montazeri also attacked the government for mismanagement and injustice. He called for a more open society in which more criticism would be permitted. He even suggested that if the government's actions compromised the values and principles of the Iranian people, it would be better not to have government.

■ Nine years after taking control of Iran, Khomeini's own grip on the country was slipping. Ayatollah Montazeri *(far right)* was critical of the government's harsh rule and mismanagement. Montazeri was once considered by Khomeini as a successor to rule the country. This soon would change.

On the morning of February 14, 1989, Khomeini reacted to the criticism. As Khomeini biographer Baqer Moin sees it, Khomeini created a confrontation with the outside world as a means of strengthening his beloved Islamic revolution at home and bolstering his claim to be leader of the entire Islamic world. He issued a *fatwa*, a religious decree having the force of law, against author Salman Rushdie. Rushdie's book *The Satanic Verses* was deemed blasphemous and had been causing rising unrest

■ Khomeini outraged both clerics in Iran and intellectuals around the world when he called for author Salman Rushdie's death in 1989. Khomeini would die of a heart attack later that same year, but the death sentence on Rushdie would last for more than a decade.

in the Muslim world for weeks. Khomeini sentenced both Rushdie and the publishers of his book to death.

Trying to defuse the situation, President Khamene'i suggested that if Rushdie apologize and disown the book, people might forgive him. In a follow-up statement, however, Khomeini left no room for compromise. A statement issued by Khomeini's office stated, "Even if Salman Rushdie repents and becomes the most pious man of all time, it is incumbent on every Muslim to employ everything he has got, his life and wealth, to send him to Hell."

Khomeini then turned back to domestic matters, writing the long "Letter to the Clergy" on February 22. The letter defended all his actions, urging the clergy to stay the course. The letter also contained several veiled assaults on Montazeri.

When, in March, the letters Montazeri had written about the purge of the prisons found their way on to BBC Radio, Khomeini had had enough. He removed Montazeri as his successor, writing him a scathing letter that at one point threatened, "If you continue your deeds I will definitely be obliged to do something about you. And you know me, I never neglect my obligation."

Montazeri resigned. His departure created a new problem: The constitution required that the leader be a marja', and there were no marja's whose political records were acceptable to Khomeini.

The solution was to amend the constitution so that Khomeini's personal choice as successor, President Ali Khamene'i, could be appointed, even though he wasn't a marja'. Three weeks after Montazeri's dismissal, Khomeini issued a decree convening a twenty-five-man Assembly of Experts to amend the constitution.

The End of the Imam

The Assembly of Experts had not yet met when Khomeini suffered a heart attack in June 1989. At about 1 PM on Saturday, June 3, he called his wife and children to his bedside. There, according to biographer Baqer Moin, he spoke his final words: "This is a very difficult path . . . Watch all your words and deeds . . . I have nothing more to add. Those who want to stay, may do so; those who don't may go. Put the light out. I want to sleep." At about 3:30 PM, he suffered a second heart attack. He had another heart attack around 10 PM and was pronounced dead at about 10:20 PM. He was eighty-six years old.

Tehran Radio officially announced the news at 7 AM on June 4. "The lofty Spirit of Allah has joined the celestial heaven," the sobbing announcer said.

The Assembly of Experts had not yet finished discussing the changes to the constitution. Realizing it

■ Mourning women stand behind their men during funeral services for Ayatollah Khomeini in June 1989. While many Iranians saw Khomeini's death as the end of his great Islamic revolution, others saw it as the end of tyranny. Nonetheless, fundamentalists took over and little changed in the country for many years.

had to announce a successor as soon as possible, they chose Ali Khamene'i, Khomeini's personal choice.

Five national days of mourning were followed by forty days of official mourning. Millions of people gathered for the funeral. The event degenerated into a frenzy in which people tore the body's shroud, seeking holy relics. Shots had to be fired into the air to force the crowd back so the body could be recovered. Better crowd control allowed the funeral to take place successfully the next

Ayatollah Khomeini

■ The frenzied response to Khomeini's death was exhibited at his funeral. Pushing and shoving to try and get at the body turned dangerous for people. Stampeding mourners killed dozens of people. Shreds of the ayatollah's death shroud were torn from the corpse to be kept as mementos.

day. Dozens of people had died, however, and more than 10,000 people were injured during the funeral and in the first few days of mourning.

Today, the most ornate shrine in Islam and one of the largest monuments ever constructed in the Muslim world rises above Khomeini's burial site south of Tehran. It has become a major tourist attraction.

The Legacy of Khomeini

Iran has continued to change in the years since Khomeini's death and not necessarily in ways that Khomeini would have approved of. Ali Khamene'i is still the leader. The current president, Mohammad Khatami, however, is a reformer who won a surprise victory in the 1997 elections. He had promised to restore the rule of law and to encourage freedom and civil society. He has faced strong opposition from the Khomeini-inspired clerical forces.

For Americans, Khomeini continues to cast a long shadow. His efforts to export his revolution have led to U.S. charges that Iran supports terrorism. Following the terrorist attacks on the World Trade Center towers in New York and the Pentagon near Washington, D.C., on September 11, 2001, President

Ayatollah Khomeini

■ Dissident clerics and student demonstrators remain prominent in Iranian society even today. Protesters here hold placards of Khomeini and his successor, Khamene'i, while protesting the outspokenness of another cleric, Ayatollah Montazeri.

George W. Bush labeled Iran, Iraq, and North Korea an "Axis of Evil."

Until then, Khatami's presidency had helped ease tensions between Iran and the United States. President Bush's statement raised new tensions and gave new life to the hard-line elements opposing Khatami's reforms. Tensions have been raised further by the United States–led invasion of Iraq, which Iranians see as renewed American imperialism in the region. It reminds them of American support for the shah's hated regime.

It is too soon to say exactly what Khomeini's legacy will be. Khomeini's Islamic revolution has endured more than two decades after its first surge. It continues to hold millions in its grip more than a decade after its leader's death. Nevertheless, Iran remains divided internally over the best way forward.

As Baqer Moin puts it, in his biography, *Khomeini: Life of the Ayatollah,* "The way an Iranian sees the revolution has been inextricably connected with the way he or she sees Khomeini, and the unraveling of these two perceptions will perhaps be the story of Iranian politics for some time to come."

1902 On September 24, Ruhollah Musavi Khomeini is born in Khomein in central Iran.

1903 In March, Ruhollah's father, Mostafa, is shot and killed.

1906 Iran's Constitutional Revolution institutes major democratic reforms. Clerical leaders who signed the new Iranian constitution are honored with the name ayatollah, which means "sign of God."

1907 Mohammad Ali Shah abolishes the Majles (parliament) and arrests the constitutional leaders.

1909 Mohammad Ali Shah is deposed and replaced by his son, Sultan Ahmad, age eleven.

1918 Ruhollah's mother and aunt die in a cholera epidemic.

1919 Ruhollah enters the madraseh, or seminary.

1921 Reza Khan and the British-sponsored Cossack Brigade help Seyyed Zia Tabataba'i overthrow the government of Premier Sepahdar Rashti. Ahmad Shah appoints Tabataba'i prime minister.

1922 Ruhollah commits himself to studying religion. He receives the turban of the talebah, or "seeker."
Ruhollah moves to Qom, ninety miles south of Tehran. He spends the next forty years there, studying and teaching.

1923 Under British pressure, Ahmad Shah names Reza Khan prime minister then leaves the country.

1925 Reza Khan becomes shah of Iran.

1929	Khomeini marries fifteen-year-old Qodse Iran.
1941	Reza Shah is forced from power by an Allied invasion at the height of the Second World War; his son Muhammad Reza, twenty-one, is given the throne.
1961	Land reform legislation results in massive unrest.
1962	Khomeini enters the political arena in response to an electoral reform proposal that would allow women and non-Muslims to vote. He begins stirring up opposition to the government and quickly becomes seen as a leader of the anti-shah elements.
1963	On June 3, Khomeini insults the shah in a speech to a large demonstration. Two days later, he is arrested.
1964	On April 7, Khomeini is released and returned to Qom. On November 4, Khomeini is arrested again and exiled to Ankara, Turkey.
1965	On January 3, Khomeini's son Mostafa joins him in exile. In October, Khomeini leaves Turkey for Najaf, Iraq. His sermons and writings while in Najaf are widely circulated in Iran.
1976	In June, pro-Khomeini groups stage a major demonstration in Qom. On October 23, Khomeini's son Mostafa dies suddenly from an apparent heart attack.

Many people think he might have been murdered by Savak.

In November, Jimmy Carter is elected president of the United States.

1977 In November, an article in a government newspaper attacking Khomeini prompts massive, violent demonstrations.

1978 On September 6–8, anti-shah demonstrations result in martial law being declared.

In October, Khomeini leaves Iraq for Paris.

On December 10 and 11, millions march in Iran, demanding the removal of the shah and the return of Khomeini.

1979 On January 16, the shah leaves Iran for good.

On February 1, Ayatollah Khomeini returns to a hero's welcome in Iran.

In April, Khomeini declares Iran an Islamic Republic.

On November 4, Iranian students take over the U.S. Embassy in Tehran and hold fifty-two Americans hostage.

1980 In January, Dr. Abol-Hasan Bani-Sadr is elected president of Iran.

On September 22, Iraq attacks western Iran. The Iran-Iraq War eventually lasts eight years.

1981 On January 20, the day of President Ronald Reagan's inauguration, the U.S. hostages are released.

On June 8, Bani-Sadr calls for "resistance to dictatorship" in a speech. After Khomeini strips him of his title of commander-in-chief and the Majles votes to impeach him, he is forced to flee the country.

1982 A plot to assassinate Khomeini is uncovered. It involved the former foreign minister Sadeq Qotbzadeh. He and as many as seventy army officers are executed.

1988 On July 3, An American warship shoots down an Iran Air flight it mistook for an attacking aircraft, killing 290 civilians. The Iranian government convinces Khomeini that he has to accept a negotiated end to the war. He agrees.

In August, Khomeini launches a purge of political prisoners. Over two months several thousand are executed.

On August 20, Iraq and Iran sign a cease-fire ending their eight-year war.

1989 In February, Ayatollah Khomeini issues a fatwa (religious decree) ordering the death of British author Salman Rushdie, whose book *The Satanic Verses* he calls blasphemous.

In March, Khomeini removes Ayatollah Hussein Ali Montazeri as his successor, in response to Montazeri's criticism of the purge of the prisons, and names Ayatollah Seyed Ali Khamene'i as his chosen replacement.

On June 4, Ayatollah Khomeini dies. Ali Khamene'i is elected as the new spiritual leader of the Islamic Republic.

ayatollah Means "sign of God"; a leading expert in Islamic law.

ayatollah al-ozma Translates as the "greatest sign of God" or the "grand ayatollah"; it is a title of respect for the leading expert in Islamic law.

faqih An expert in the law.

fatwa An opinion or decree passed down by an Islamic religious leader.

hajj The annual pilgrimage to Mecca. Every sane, financially able, adult Muslim is required by Islamic law to make hajj at least once.

hojjat al-Islam Means the "proof of Islam"; this was originally a title of high respect, equivalent to today's ayatollah, and is now used for any cleric.

imam This is one of the twelve successors of the Prophet descended from Ali. In Arabic, it means any learned cleric.

jihad A holy war or defense of the faith.

khan A chieftain.

madraseh Translates as a "place of learning;" an Islamic religious seminary, equivalent to a university for the study of Islamic law.

Majles Short for Majles-e Showra-ye Melli; the Iranian parliament.

maktab A religious elementary school.

marja' taqlid The supreme authority on the law.

mojtahed An Islamic jurist who is permitted to issue his own opinions on legal matters.

mosque A place of worship.

mullah An older term for a cleric.

mysticism The belief that direct knowledge of God can be attained through individual insight or inspiration.

Savak The secret police of the shah of Iran.

shah The king of Iran.

shari'a The law of Islam.

Shiism The smaller of the two main branches of modern Islam, made up of descendants of people who backed the prophet Muhammad's nephew Ali as successor to the Prophet after the Prophet's death in 632.

Sunnism The larger of the two main branches of modern Islam, made up of descendants of people who accepted a leader from outside the Prophet's family after his death in 632.

talebah Means a "seeker after knowledge" or a religious student.

taqiyya "Dissimulation"; a doctrine that allows Shiite Muslims to go so far as to pretend to abandon their faith in order to continue practicing it.

valiy-e faqih In the Islamic state as envisioned by Khomeini, the leading cleric and therefore the leader of the country. Khomeini was valiy-e faqih while he was alive; currently, the valiy-e faqih is Ali Khamene'i.

velayat-e faqih "The governance of the jurist"; Khomeini's theory of Islamic government, which puts experts in Islamic law in control of legislation.

ORGANIZATIONS

The American Institute of Iranian Studies
Executive Director
118 Riverside Drive
New York, NY 10024
e-mail: aiis@nyc.rr.com
Web site: http://www.simorgh-aiis.org

American Iranian Council
20 Nassau Street, Suite 111
Princeton, NJ 08542
(609) 252-9099
e-mail: aic@american-iranian.org
Web site: http://www.american-iranian.org

Foundation for Iranian Studies
4343 Montgomery Avenue
Bethesda, MD 20814
(301) 657-1990
e-mail: fis@fis-iran.org
Web site: http://www.fis-iran.org

The Society for Iranian Studies
Department of Middle Eastern Studies
New York University
50 Washington Square South
New York, NY 10012
Web site: http://www.iranian-studies.org

WEB SITES

Due to the changing nature of Internet links, the Rosen Publishing Group, Inc., has developed an online list of Web sites related to the subject of this book. This site is updated regularly. Please use this link to access the list:

http://www.rosenlinks.com/mel/akho

Cartlidge, Cherese. *Iran*. San Diego, CA: Lucent
    Books, 2002.

Gordon, Matthew S. *Ayatollah Khomeini*. Broomall,
    PA: Chelsea House Publishers, 1987.

Penney, Sue. *Islam*. Barrington, IL: Heinemann
    Library, 2000.

Rajendra, Vijeya, and Gisela T. Kaplan. *Iran:
    Cultures of the World*. New York: Benchmark
    Books, 1995.

Spencer, William. *Islamic Fundamentalism in the
    Modern World*. Brookfield, CT: Millbrook
    Press, 1995.

Spencer, William. *The United States and Iran*.
    New York: Twenty-first Century Books, 2000.

BIBLIOGRAPHY

Algar, Hamid. "Imam Khomeini: A Brief Biography."
    Retrieved April 24, 2003 (http://www.msapsg.org/
    imam99/algar/imambio0.htm).

Arjomand, Said Amir. *The Turban for the Crown:
    The Islamic Revolution in Iran*. New York:
    Oxford University Press, 1988.

Bakhash, Shaul. *The Reign of the Ayatollahs: Iran
    and the Islamic Revolution*. New York: Basic
    Books, 1984.

Fischer, Michael M. J. *Iran: From Religious Dispute
    to Revolution*. Cambridge, MA: Harvard
    University Press, 1980.

Milani, Mohsen M. *The Making of Iran's Islamic
    Revolution: From Monarchy to Islamic
    Republic*. Boulder, CO: Westview Press, 1988.

Moin, Baqer. *Khomeini: Life of the Ayatollah*.
    New York: Thomas Dunne Books, 1999.

Stempel, John D. *Inside the Iranian Revolution*.
    Bloomington, IN: Indiana University Press, 1981.

Wright, Robin B. *The Last Great Revolution: Turmoil
    and Transformation in Iran*. New York: Alfred
    A. Knopf, 2000.

INDEX

About the Author

Edward Willett is the author of more than twenty books, ranging from children's nonfiction books to computer books to young adult science fiction and fantasy novels. He is also a professional actor and singer. He lives in Saskatchewan, Canada.

Photo Credits

Front cover map, pp. 3 (chapter 3 box), 6–7, 10–11, 12–13, 40, 80–81 © Perry-Castãnedia Library Map Collection/The University of Texas at Austin; front cover image, pp. 3 (chapter 1 and 5 boxes), 75, 76, 88–89, 96–97 © AP/Wide World Photos; flags on back cover and on pp. 1, 3, 4, 8, 16, 26, 46, 66, 100, 102, 104, 106, 108, 109, 110 © Nelson Sá; pp. 1, 4, 24, 31, 32–33, 38–39 © Hulton/Archive/ Getty Images; pp. 3 (chapter 2 box), 22, 28, 83 © Corbis; pp. 3 (chapter 4 box), 20–21, 26, 34–35, 37, 44–45, 46, 49, 50–51, 53, 57, 58–59, 60, 62–63, 66, 68–69, 70, 73 © Bettmann/Corbis; pp. 8, 91 © Vahid Salemi/AP/Wide World Photos; p. 16 © Paul Almasy/Corbis; p. 18 © Hulton-Deutsch/Corbis; p. 55 © Roger Wood/Corbis; p. 82 © Maher Attar/Corbis; pp. 84–85 © Reza/Webistan/Corbis; pp. 92–93 © Enric Marti/AP/Wide World Photos; p. 95 © Reuters New Media Inc./Corbis; p. 98 © Mohammad Sayyad/AP/Wide World Photos.

Designer: Nelson Sá; **Editor:** Mark Beyer;
Photo Researcher: Nelson Sá